Synopsis

of

Live Not By Lies (A Manual for Christian Dissidents)

By Rod Dreher
Genius Reads

Note to Readers:

This is an unofficial summary & analysis of Rod Dreher's {"Live Not By Lies (A Manual for Christian Dissidents)"} designed to enrich your reading experience.

Legal & Disclaimer

The information contained in this book and its contents is not designed to replace or take the place of any form of medical or professional advice; and is not meant to replace the need for independent medical, financial, legal, or other professional advice or services, as may be required. The content and information in this book have been provided for educational and entertainment purposes only.

The content and information contained in this book have been compiled from sources deemed reliable, and it is accurate to the best of the Author's knowledge, information, and belief. However, the Author cannot guarantee its accuracy and validity and cannot be held liable for any errors and/or omissions. Further, changes are periodically made to this book as and when needed. Where appropriate and/or necessary, you must consult a professional (including but not limited to your doctor, attorney, financial advisor, or such other professional advisor) before using any of the suggested remedies, techniques, or information in this book.

Upon using the contents and information contained in this book, you agree to hold harmless the Author from and against any damages, costs, and expenses, including any legal fees potentially resulting from the application of any of the information provided by this book. This disclaimer applies to any loss, damages, or injury caused by the use and application, whether directly or indirectly, of any advice or information presented, whether for breach of contract, tort, negligence, personal injury, criminal intent, or under any other cause of action.

You agree to accept all risks of using the information presented inside this book.

You agree that by continuing to read this book, where appropriate and/or necessary, you shall consult a professional (including but not limited to your doctor, attorney, or financial advisor or such other advisor as needed) before using any of the suggested remedies, techniques, or information in this book.

Download Your Free Gift

Before you go any further, why not pick up a free gift from me to you?

Smarter Brain – a 10-part video training series to help you develop higher IQ, memory, and creativity – FAST!

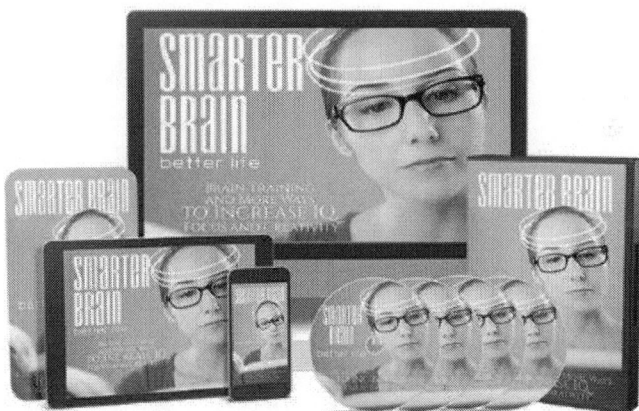
A SUMMARY OF

Live Not By Lies (A Manual For Christian Dissidents) By Rod Dreher

TABLE OF CONTENTS

PART TWO: How To Live In Truth

CHAPTER FIVE

☐   Value Nothing More Than the Truth

☐   Choose A Life Apart From The Crowd

☐   Reject Doublethink and Fight for Free Speech

☐   Cherish Truth-Telling But Be Prudent

☐   See, Judge, Act

CHAPTER SIX

☐   Cultivate Cultural Memory

☐   Why Memory Matters

☐   Create Small Fortresses of Memory

☐   Make the Parallel Polis into Sanctuary Cities

☐   Bear Communal Witness to Future Generations

☐   See, Judge, Act

9

□   God's Saboteurs

SUMMARY

Penned by noted American conservative figure Rod
Dreher, Live Not by Lies (A Manual for Christian
Dissidents) is about the rise of a new kind of
totalitarianism in America. It is divided into 2 Parts,
unfolding over 10 Chapters and bookended by an
Introduction and Conclusion.

Part One is called "Understanding Soft
Totalitarianism". It explains what totalitarianism is,
and how it has evolved over the last 30 years.
Dreher provides the historical context, origins and
process of his research, and differentiates soft
totalitarianism from its more recognizable
predecessor, hard totalitarianism. He discusses why
soft totalitarianism has gone unnoticed and
unchecked in democratic societies, and the signs
that prove its existence and growth in America. He
also talks about woke culture and how it creates an
"ideological fog" for people to get lost into,
disguised in form and language as a progressive
liberator of the oppressed, and a deliverer of justice.
Combined with a growing faithless/godless culture,
nurtured by unfettered capitalism focused on the
pursuit of pleasure and convenience, and supported
by technological advancements, the Left is

succeeding in its agenda to make pliable people out of its citizens, in order to control them.

He lays the foundation for Part Two, titled "How-to Live-in Truth". He shows his reader how to practice "living in truth", the only weapon in the fight to resist soft totalitarianism in everyday life. He stresses the importance of ensuring younger generations are fully aware of the horrors of a totalitarian society, and how close a threat it still is, even in a country like the US. Dreher elaborates on the role religious faith plays in the battle against this unseen and insidious evil. He challenges his reader to take up the call to "intellectual" arms, to stop its spread by firmly anchoring oneself to the teachings of the Christian faith and to stand firm on one's deeply held conservative convictions. In short, to live not by lies, but by the truth.

A narrative told in the first person, Rod Dreher's Live Not by Lies (A Manual for Christian Dissidents) is both condensed lecture and cautionary tale, history lesson and present-day guidebook. It is a full-bodied discussion, much like wine that had been aging for some time and finally opened, allowed to breathe and decanted.

Aimed at the ordinary (preferably) Christian conservative reader, Rod Dreher writes in as plain a language as possible, sharing the lens of his personal observations, and drawn conclusions. The book rises above being just an extended and elaborate political commentary and reading it is like having a passionate and engaging discussion about the socio-political realities of the world today. It's personal and one feels the strength of Dreher's conviction and concern, as he builds up to the book's ultimate goal: to provide a life-manual – of the mind-setting, choice-informing kind, on how one could conduct everyday life in valiant resistance against the forces of totalitarianism – which Dreher convinces are already a present threat in American society.

INTRODUCTION

In the spring of 2015, Rod Dreher, noted conservative public figure and author of Live Not by Lies (A Manual for Christian Dissidents) received an alarming phone call from a stranger. An American doctor whose mother, a 90-year-old Czechoslovakian immigrant who spent 6 years in prison in her homeland as an anti-communist Catholic dissident, talked to her son about how recent events unfolding reminded her of the beginnings of communism in Czechoslovakia.

The specific incident that prompted this was the social media storm that surrounded a pizzeria in Indiana. Its Christian owners had refused to cater to a same-sex wedding, and they received so many threats as a result they were forced to temporarily close shop. Something about the doctor's tone rattled Dreher. The man who spoke to him with urgency was raised by immigrant parents who fought and fled communism in their youth. And while that upbringing came with constant warnings to be vigilant about the spread of totalitarianism in society, the doctor never took it seriously. He didn't worry it could happen in the USA. But the pizzeria incident rocked him from this secure perch.

This is how Rod Dreher introduces his readers to his book Live Not by Lies (A Manual for Christian Dissidents), explaining the why and how of its origins.

He starts by talking about how the Fall of the Berlin Wall in 1989 may have put his generation and those that followed under a false sense of complacency. Certain that the threat of Soviet totalitarianism has been quashed, democratic societies like the US believed that the age of democracy and capitalism was about to flourish. But the phone call he received from the agitated physician served as a wake-up call. What if that doctor's mother was right? What if, unnoticed, the rise of totalitarianism had already begun in the "land of the free"?

Over the next few years, Rod Dreher began interviewing people who had lived under communist Soviet states to ask them what they thought about the fears raised by the doctor's mother. All of them agreed strongly with her observations and pointed out the similarities between the beginnings of totalitarianism in Russia and what's happening now in America.

Powerful institutions shifted from the belief of defending individual rights (traditional liberalism) to a new, progressive values system, that wants individuals to identify with Groups based on race, sexual identity and other personality markers. These Groups define for society what is Good and what is Evil, depending on which Group holds the most power. Dreher calls these powerful entities "utopian progressives" and they are fueled by a utopian vision of society, for which they will rewrite history, invent new language and most troubling, constantly revise the rules of what is acceptable behavior.

The consequences of misaligning with or challenging these changing values are dire, like loss of livelihood, destroyed reputations and ostracism from society. Part of the problem is that America thinks totalitarianism always looks like its depiction in the Soviet states: oppressive, bloody, immiserating. America lives so freely by comparison that it can't believe the idea that totalitarianism is here and growing. Further, the language of the Left is designed to make one believe that the ideology they stand on is against oppression. Words like equality, inclusivity, diversity is mere " egalitarian jargon" used to disguise the end goal which is to police thought and vilify anyone in opposition. Conservative views, they noted, have become so unappealing that even expressing them feels dangerous and requires one to be discreet and careful.

Rod Dreher's Live Not by Lies also connects the role religion (Christianity in particular) plays in arresting the spread of totalitarianism in society. Religion being its mortal enemy, Christianity had to be eradicated by communist states. But while the old face of totalitarianism did so with bloody force, the same is happening now in countries like the US, albeit hidden inside a new and softer version. Progressive and anti-Christian ideology is growing, proven by the large numbers of people born within the last 40 years in the Western world, rejecting religious faith. Pope Benedict XVI described this societal re-formation as "the worldwide dictatorship of humanistic ideologies" where the spiritual power of the Anti-Christ is manifested.

Subtly enforced by all sectors of society, it is boosted by technological advancements which marginalize those who still adhere to traditional and/or religious, faith-based values. And when living in a society with a growing majority without spiritual anchor, Christians become more vulnerable to attack because that society will have become increasingly intolerant of religious, faith-based dissent

Rod Dreher talks about Alexander Solzhenitsyn, the famed anti-communist dissident, who was exiled by Russia after he published The Gulag Archipelago, which exposed the horrors of Soviet totalitarianism and gained him global hero status. According to Solzhenitsyn, communism was created and sustained not so much by a political crisis but a spiritual one. The only way to combat the coming threat of soft totalitarianism is to strengthen one's spiritual life.

Before he left his homeland, Alexander published one final letter addressed to his countrymen. An essay entitled "Live Not by Lies" which challenged the idea that Soviet totalitarianism -- cannot be challenged. According to Solzhenitsyn, the foundation of totalitarianism is an ideology made of lies. The antidote then is to live in truth, in direct opposition to everything totalitarianism stands for.

Defying a totalitarian state's rule need not be a public act. The simple rejection of the lies fed by the government, and finding ways to live in truth with dignity, is already a triumph.

Rod Dreher, by way of concluding the Introduction, presents to the reader the fundamental question he tries to answer in the book. What does it mean in the present time, to live NOT by lies? Conversely how does one live a life of truth?

In these troubled times, it has never been more relevant to ask these questions.

PART ONE

Understanding Soft Totalitarianism

-

CHAPTER ONE

Kolakovic the Prophet

Rod Dreher opens Chapter 1 of Live Not by Lies (A Manual for Christian Dissidents) with the inspirational story of Father Kolakovic, a Jesuit priest in Czechoslovakia during WW2 who, after correctly foreseeing how Soviet totalitarianism could devastate the Catholic faithful, acted to prepare his flock and strengthen them for the trials to come when the country inevitably came under communist rule.

Tomislav Poglajen was a 37-year-old Jesuit priest and anti-fascist activist who escaped Croatia in 1943. He settled in Czechoslovakia, took his Slovak mother's name "Kolakovic" and became a teacher in the Slovak capital of Bratislava. When the Soviets defeated the Germans in 1944, the exiled

Czechoslovakian government which also
represented Slovakia, entered into a deal with Stalin,
who promised that once the Nazis were out, the
Soviets would give the reunited nations their
freedom.

Having studied Soviet totalitarianism when he was
a priest in training, Father Kolakovic foresaw this to
be the lie it ultimately proved to be. He warned his
flock that when the war was over, the country
would come under Soviet communist rule through a
puppet government.

Father Kolakovic took inspiration from the Young
Christian Workers or Jocists, a lay movement
started by Belgian priest Joseph Cardjin, and
adapted his methods in Slovakia, establishing cells
of devout young Catholics who could "gather for
prayer, study and fellowship." He called them his
"Family" and they embraced the Jocists' motto:
"See. Judge. Act".

The Family gathered to pray, study Scripture and
listen to Father Kolakovic lecture on a variety of
intellectual subjects. Additionally, Father Kolakovic
taught his young followers the clandestine arts of

22

resistance, including how to work secretly, and how to endure an interrogation.

It was an underground Church movement that grew and spread quickly across the nation.

By 1944, after only a year, there was hardly an academic institution in Bratislava or in other major cities where you couldn't find circles of The Family in action.

The Czechoslovakian government deported Father Kolakovic two years later and in 1948, the Soviet communists took power as he predicted. The Church was forced into submission by the State, and The Family was decimated, with nearly all members sent to prison within a few short years.

Yet in the 1960s, when they got out, members immediately went about the task of quietly rebuilding the underground Church, led by the priest's top 2 lieutenants, Dr. Silvester Krčméry, and Fr. Vladimír Jukl.

Rod Dreher calls Father Kolakovic a visionary cleric whose spiritual progeny following his teachings, (re)built the faith-based movement that would become the foundation of anti-communist dissent in Czechoslovakia for the next 4 decades. It was The Family who organized The Candle Revolution, a mass protest in 1988 in Bratislava, demanding religious freedom. This kindled the Velvet Revolution which peacefully toppled the communist regime one year later. One priest's faith, foresight and spiritual strength laid the groundwork for a thriving Catholic Church in Czechoslovakia, despite the fact of Slovak Christians being the most persecuted under Soviet rule at the time.

Father Kolakovic saw what was coming and prepared his flock. And that act eventually won for their country, freedom.

The New Totalitarianism

Father Kolakovic used his background and experience (early studies of Soviet communism, familiarity with organized resistance) to do and foresee the things he did, and to take action. In today's society, the survivors of Soviet communism are our modern day Kolakovices. And much like the Jesuit priest, they are warning us that a new totalitarianism is coming. Totalitarianism is a type of government that wields the combined power of political authoritarianism and ideological control.

What's troubling about the "new" totalitarianism is that it isn't easily recognizable. It differs in form from the one society is more familiar with— armed, harsh and enforced with gulags. This is the Soviet's template for "hard" totalitarianism.

The form that is creeping unnoticed into democratic societies like the US is gentler, softer— Dreher even uses the word "therapeutic" to describe it. And this softer version hates dissent just as much but conceals it behind a facade of compassion and intent of healing.

Dreher explains that to appreciate the gravity of its threat, one must understand the difference between totalitarianism and simple authoritarian rule. The latter is a government with complete and unopposed political control, often characterized as a dictatorship. Totalitarianism is worse. He references Hannah Arendt, the foremost scholar on the subject, who says totalitarianism wants to control all of society under a singular ideology. A totalitarian state's ultimate goal is to "define and control reality" for the people. And that reality, that truth or ideology — is whatever the current rulers decide it to be. More than just controlling reality, totalitarianism also wants to control thoughts and emotions. Love for the Party was required of the people during the Soviet era, which bred compliance with Party demands which were then enforced by the State. Now in soft totalitarianism, the Party has been replaced by a set of Progressive Beliefs that people must give allegiance to, and the state has a new face for enforcing compliance, in the Elites who have become Opinion Makers, and Private Corporations enabled by technology to control our lives.

Conservative society remains dismissive of this threat. Most equate present day manifestations of it with the same left-wing "campus kookiness" in the 90s. But that generation brought that "campus kookiness" to nearly every sector in society today. It has become a cultural revolution where they attempt to turn the country "into a "woke" college campus". And people who dissent, who break away from the "woke party line" are demonized, ostracized and cancelled, their lives and livelihoods destroyed.

The Gentleness of Soft Totalitarianism

In this section, Dreher talks about the veil worn by soft totalitarianism, and how people miss it for lack of understanding of its power workings.

In "The Captive Mind", author Czesław Miłosz, a poet and literary critic from Poland who was exiled to the West for being an anti-communist dissident, says most people equate communism with "might and coercion", which is why its nature—as well as its appeal— is misunderstood.

The human desire for harmony and happiness outweighs "ordinary fear, desire to escape misery and physical destruction." He points out that communist ideology filled a void for a lot of early 20th century intellectuals, most of whom no longer believed in religion. Today, that same void manifests as a deep hunger for a just society, one that tries to "vindicate and liberate historical victims of oppression."

Totalitarianism hides behind the language of compassion and empathy expressed by left wing progressives who identify dissenters from "disfavored demographics" who are then demonized, shunned, and "cancelled" as victimizers and oppressors. Dreher calls them SJWs or social justice warriors, one-time true compassionate liberals whose rabid cause for social justice has seen them exchange authentic liberalism for an "aggressive, punitive politics" that closely resembles Bolshevism: what communism was first called in Russia.

This is the warning of communism survivors to the democratic West— to stop the spread of this destructive ideology that began as a noble cause by liberals to protect "the weak and the marginalized". Or else watch liberal democracy yield to "a soft and therapeutic totalitarianism."

The Therapeutic as the Postmodern Mode of Existence

Soft totalitarianism will not have a hard time settling in democratic society. Modern man is decadent, and values comfort and convenience so much he is willing to sacrifice principles and political freedoms for it. Aldous Huxley's "Brave New World" more accurately paints this near-future picture than Orwell's "1984".

28

The Pink Police State, as coined by critic James Poulos, is an unspoken arrangement between the people and the state where the former willingly gives up its rights in exchange for pleasure.

Personal well-being became man and society's ultimate goal, attributable to the death of God in the West. This is according to noted American sociologist and cultural critic Philip Rieff who wrote The Triumph of the Therapeutic in 1966. He explains how postmodern civilization set man free to pursue his own happiness unencumbered by rules or any transcendental order.

It gave birth to the Psychological Man, replacing the Religious Man. Whereas the latter lived a life following divine principles that served a communal purpose, the former believes every man must live his life his own way, governed only by the pursuit of personal happiness. According to Rieff this notion is even more radical than the Bolshevik event of 1917, whose revolutionaries, while godless, still believed in a metaphysical order where man was bound to sacrifice personal desires to serve a bigger purpose.

He predicted that the West would crush communism with this therapeutic ideological revolution. It freed man to pursue whatever he wished, without submission to a sacred order, rendering him as a god unto himself.

But Rieff saw that without a shared belief binding its believers, an "anti-culture culture" is formed, which is inherently unstable. He also predicted that religious society under this therapeutic ideology would result in a diluted spirituality, where anything is permissible. In the words of religion sociologists Christian Smith and Melinda Denton, who coined "Moralistic Therapeutic Deism", America has defined God as a being who "only wants man to be nice and happy."

Post 1960s, the conversational focus of the radical Left shifted from economic class struggle to sexual revolution and ethnic and gender identity politics. Which isn't surprising in therapeutic culture, where man's freedom to pursue happiness is his righteous right. This new culture also found a natural ally in advanced capitalism, which follows a prime directive to satisfy human desires. The religious Right likewise accepted the therapeutic ideology, following the Cold War and the cultural upheavals of the '60s and '70s. Christian conservatives thought religion could be reformed along the lines of this new culture, since the true definition of freedom is now freedom of choice as opposed to "choosing virtue". And because therapeutic society deems suffering of man as needless, Christianity would and has failed to combat this anti-culture revolution. Because why suffer for the faith, if suffering has no purpose?

Ketman And the Pill of Murti Bing

Communism rests on multiple layers of lies, founded on the primordial lie that there is only ONE source of truth- the state. He references Orwell who said in "1984": "The Party told you to reject the evidence of your eyes and ears. It was their final, most essential command."

He talks further of language and jargon called "newspeak" and "doublethink", devices invented by the Party to control how the people think, to such a degree that citizens would believe whatever information is fed to them even if all their senses, the most basic being common sense, contradicts it.

This forceful state brainwashing won't happen in our time, in America. Soft totalitarianism operates on a subtler frequency, utilizing all the main institutions in society to engage in their own "newspeak", compel us to "doublethink" , and condition us to subscribe to ideologies that run counter to basic logic. Dreher cites as examples calling a woman "he", men having periods, and that inclusion is exclusion of those who don't believe in inclusion etc.

Many Christian conservatives stay silent despite being aware that this is happening in society. According to our Polish dissident writer Milosz, this will only corrode them.

He cites Insatiability, a 1932 novel by another Polish writer Stanislaw Wietkewicz. His story is of a dystopian future where people are "culturally exhausted and have fallen into decadence" and now a Mongol army wants to overrun them. To do this quickly, they sold pills on the streets called "Murti Bing" named after a Mongolian philosopher who found a way to make into a tablet his motto of "don't worry, be happy". People started taking the pills, became worry-free about life and when the invaders from the east came, they surrendered without resistance. But when the pills wore off their

32

former personas would emerge. Milosz writes "They became schizophrenic." People become actors and practice "ketman" — a Persian word that means maintaining an "outward appearance of Islamic orthodoxy while inwardly dissenting." Ketman was how you survived communism if you were not a true believer but wanted to stay out of trouble. But it's corrosive, Milosz points out, and worse than hypocrisy. Living with it all the time inevitably destroys you inside. Dreher says that many conservatives including Christians today practice ketman in one form or more, in their daily lives. And there are those who reach a level of self-deception so deep they've convinced themselves that they can live within "woke systems" honestly, while changing and adapting their convictions to suit the new order.

Live in Truth

In this section Rod Dreher talks about Alexander Solzhenitsyn who is likely one of the great inspirations of his book Live Not by Lies (A Manual for Christian Dissidents). Dreher writes that before he was arrested Alexander published one final letter addressed to his countrymen. An essay entitled "Live Not by Lies" which challenged the idea that Soviet totalitarianism cannot be challenged, at least not by the ordinary citizen.

He says that since the foundation of totalitarianism is an ideology made of lies, the antidote is to live in truth, in direct opposition to everything totalitarianism stands for.

Defying a totalitarian state's rule need not be a public act. By the simple rejection of the lies fed by the government, and finding in oneself and community, even a silent way to live in truth with dignity, is a triumph.

Alexander says that even if one has to live under their regime, one can forbid the rule of the communist State to live through one's life. He even provides a list of doable acts to concretize this refusal to live by lies. Dreher ends by saying the task of today's Christian dissident is to live not by lies. That one should do this within a community, and following the example of Father Kolakovic, find true spiritual leadership among the lay and the clergy. One should form cells of believers to spend time with, in worship, fellowship and discussion of the struggles facing Christian believers today. These cells should practice the Jocists motto of see, judge

34

and act. In the fight against soft totalitarianism, Christian dissidents must think and act as if they are heirs of Father Kolakovic's The Family and spread out through the nation, uniting fellow believers and dissidents and "prepare for the coming suffering and resistance."

CHAPTER TWO

Our Pre-Totalitarian Culture

Rod Dreher, author of Live Not by Lies (A Manual for Christian Dissidents) devotes much of Chapter 2 to giving a historical perspective on the beginnings of totalitarianism and what precipitated it in Russia. He also notes that this history is more relevant to American society today, than most people think.

Dreher tells the story of a conversation he once had while having dinner with a Russian family in Moscow. They were talking about Soviet oppression and Dreher remarked that he couldn't understand how anyone could have believed the promises made by the Bolsheviks. The Russian father then proceeded to take him through 300 years of Russian history, ending with the 1917 Bolshevik revolt. He told Dreher in the end that while it did not excuse nor diminish the fact of the Bolsheviks' evil, it does explain where they were coming from—which was misery of the acutest kind, under the insensitive, cruel and ultimately incompetent rule of the Imperial Russian government.

There was so much suffering that the Russian revolutionary generation were ready to embrace anything that promised a way out of the muck, towards a better life. And this came in the form of communism, offered and enforced by the Bolsheviks.

While it was true that Russia became a world power under Romanov rule, it was falling apart by the turn of the 20th century. Its agricultural economy and peasantry were hopelessly stuck in backwardness as its neighbors began industrializing. Its seeming tipping point was the severe famine of 1891 which revealed how weak the Tsarist system was and how incapable the imperial government was of caring for its people.

By the end of the century, industrialization created a huge mass of underclass laborers who were exploited, oppressed and miserable. They lived in the cities, separated from their villages, families, traditions and church communities. Outside of the Tsar's bubble in the royal court, few people still believed that the system could carry on. And still the advisers of Tsar Nicholas II insisted that sticking with the traditional autocratic system was the way to survive the crisis. Calls for reform went unheeded, which included the leaders of the Russian Orthodox church whose priests were sounding the alarm that the clergy was losing sway with the people.

Meanwhile Russia's intellectuals and artists were under the spell of Prometheanism, which believed man had godlike abilities to make the world suit himself. Unrest grew with discontent, and the rest is a bloody, horrifying, totalitarian history, which no one could have imagined was coming. Not just the Tsarists but Russia's liberal minds as well.

Why Communism Appealed to Russians

In this section Rod Dreher talks about Karl Marx, the ideology he gave birth to and the role it played in the events leading to the Bolshevik revolt and beyond, as it shaped the face of communist-totalitarian Russia.

Stripped to the core, Marxism is a philosophy anchored on the belief that the world's ills are rooted in the class struggle between the rich and poor, with the latter continuously exploited by the former. And religion, according to Karl Marx, was the "opium of the people" which numbed and blinded them to endure the suffering and oppression resulting from this struggle.

He envisioned a society where power lies in the hands of the working class instead of the rich capitalists, run by a government that worked only to ensure the fair and even distribution of wealth.

Marx also believed his teachings were based on science, which coincided with the 19th century trend of European intellectuals submitting more to Science as an authority than Religion.

In the golden age of European liberalism, Russia was falling behind its neighbors, who were modernizing and industrializing. And while other autocrats were struggling to adapt their rule to more constitutional systems of governance, Russia refused to reform. Russia was suffering a steady economic decline towards the end of the 20th century, without arrest or relief given by the Imperial government. This made Marxism appealing to many of Russia's young intellectuals.

They were ashamed that their predecessors failed to change the system despite the worsening state of the country. They were done with the old ways and were restless and desperate for change. Marxism gave them the answer. They began spreading its gospel, radicalizing universities then moving to laborers and the working classes.

They promised a land of "milk and honey" that would follow a revolution to get rid of the ruling class, preaching with religious zeal that Marxism was the future of progress and justice.

Discontent within the military following the defeat of Russia against Japan allowed for waves of civil unrest to grip the nation in 1905. Russia's defeat in the Great War in 1914 sealed its fate. Led by Vladimir Lenin, the bloody October Revolution arrived in 1917 and toppled the imperial government.

Evangelizing Russia's Neighbors

Aside from the fact that the Soviets forced it, living and changing cultural conditions allowed communist and totalitarian rule to flourish in Eastern Europe in the early 20th century. Many countries in Eastern Europe were facing economic and social decline in the early 20th century. Ravaged by two Great Wars, people were wont to surrender to the invading communist ideologies powered by the Soviet forces, out of sheer psychological and economic exhaustion and pressure.

Much like the pre-revolutionary Russian intellectuals, many believed in the promised reforms of communist ideology. Patrik Benda. a political consultant, says that long before communist power rose, intellectuals and artists had already paved the way for it, as they advocated for communist ideals and excluded voices that opposed it.

The whole of Eastern Europe fell under communist dictatorships, backed by Soviet rule. And suppression of free speech, complete economic submission and religious persecution were just some of the consequences many people suffered during this time.

Dreher tells the reader that despite the fact that communism and totalitarianism were enforced and sustained through force and terror by the Soviets, there was hardship, and hopelessness, enough for people to believe in the utopian promises of communism and see it as salvation.

And under the right circumstances it can also happen in the US. While they are not exact, the events that led to the rise of communism in Eastern Europe is close to what is happening now in American society as it goes through "social, economic and institutional" decline.

It doesn't help that the US government's failure to address the Covid 19 pandemic calls to mind the way Tsar Nicholas II handled—or didn't handle, the great famine of 1891 in Imperial Russia.

Classic liberalism is dying in the Western world without a clear ideological successor. And it is ripe for the coming of a new kind of totalitarianism. Yes, democratic society today would likely shun the idea of Marxism as the solution to the world's problems. But it must remain vigilant.

How to See Totalitarianism Coming

Rod Dreher turns to scholar Hannah Arendt to understand the social conditions a person would have to be living in to create the mindset that makes him willingly submit to an ideology like totalitarianism.

Arendt, a political theorist, wrote The Origins of Totalitarianism published in 1951. She identified 6 of these conditions from studying what happened between Germany and the Soviet Union, and the prevailing social psyche that became fertile ground for activists to plant radical ideologies at the time. Rod Dreher argues that these same conditions are present in American society today.

1)   Loneliness and Social Atomization – Totalitarian ideology appeals most to people who are searching for a sense of community, solidarity and meaning. Loneliness has become a commonplace, everyday reality for many people, which has conditioned society to be more accepting of a totalitarian system. In present-day America, loneliness is regarded as a social and even medical problem that not even social media has arrested. People are more isolated, spending less time in groups or participating in civic activities. This loneliness and isolation will have political repercussions and it's not surprising that young people are drawn to ideologies and politics that can "replace the communities they wish they had."

2)   Losing Faith in Hierarchies and Institutions - In the 1920s, Arendt says totalitarianism was heralded by the failure of political parties to get younger members, as well as the masses, entertaining radical ideas to discredit establishment parties. Loss of faith in democratic entities is a sign of an unstable and weak society. Studies have shown that Americans today have lost faith in

almost all democratic institutions. People no longer look to the outside for guidance and meaning, which puts a psychological burden on individuals who may then embrace ideologies that offer solidarity and certainty, like totalitarian movements.

3)   The Desire to Transgress and Destroy – According to Arendt, writers and artists post-WW1 had much contempt for the traditional establishment and were all about anti-culture philosophy. But they did not ground their transgressive actions on any "respectable" theory and simply acted as they wished and called it liberation. Dreher likens the elites Arendt referred to in postwar history to present-day voices who ignore liberal ideas like "fair play, free speech and race neutrality as obstacles to equality." Dreher also discusses sexual transgressiveness, and how it is not a result of the sexual revolution in the West. Historians noted late Imperial Russia was as preoccupied with sex, and sexual adventurism was fairly common. Historian James Billington notes that in the age of sensualism Satan literally became a Romantic hero for artists and musicians, for representing man's will to pursue that which he desires.

4)   Propaganda & The Willingness to Believe Useful Lies - Heda Margolius Kovaly, a Czech

communist whose husband was executed in 1952, said it is easy for people to abandon the truth for an ideological cause. This is why keeping the people ignorant is easy for a totalitarian regime. Once you surrender your freedom for the sake of whatever greater cause you were sold on, all claims to the truth are forfeited.

Hannah Arendt says people in pre-totalitarian societies were prone to pretend agreement with an ideology they actually opposed, because it served the satisfying purpose of punishing those they hate. Dreher references the "1619 Project" by the NY Times, which sought to reframe the history of America's foundation through a lens of racial hatred. Despite the project's core premise being debunked, the creator was awarded a Pulitzer Prize, giving it legitimacy and prestige. Dreher talks about propaganda and how its power lies in the ability to create a false reality for people. And according to Arendt, totalitarian propaganda's power lies in its ability to shut people off from reality. Today, mainstream media and social media are working together to frame how we see the world, and "condition us to accept as true whatever feels right to us."

5)   A Mania for Ideology - To answer the question of why people are willing to believe lies, Arendt talks about man's desperation in his alienated life. He will cling to anything, any ideology or story that can provide meaning and guidance in his life. To this end, totalitarian ideology can feel like salvation. Kovaly uses her own experience of when she and her husband made the decision to become communists, saying they were looking for a way out of the hell they were living in and communism promised "paradise on earth".

Believers of an ideology always start out as idealists. Dreher also discusses how a popular phrase used by the Left today "the personal is political" captures the spirit of totalitarianism. Increasingly, Dreher says, the Left is pushing its ideology into our personal lives, which Arendt says is a sign of society "ripening" for totalitarianism. Because that is what the ideology is about, "the politicization of everything."

6)   A Society That Values Loyalty More Than Expertise - In a totalitarian society, loyalty is the most prized trait. Arendt says totalitarian powers will often replace qualified, intelligent, creative and

talented experts with people who are none of these, which keeps them loyal to the state.

Dreher uses Trump as an example of a leader who has gone on record to say loyalty is the quality he values above all else. But he scoffs at the Left who complain of this, remarking that loyalty is the core of Leftist political ideology. Cancel culture is rooted in leftist-loyalist ideology. Institutions like universities and big corporations have also found ways to identify and remove dissenters by implementing tests within their systems to find out where an employee's loyalties lie or if an actor is loyal to the ideologies it supports. As an example, Dreher reveals that allegiance to diversity is a common loyalty test in many American companies. In California, the requirements for teachers working in the UC system and applying for tenure include affirming "commitment to diversity, equity and inclusion" and to have proof of action, despite it not having anything to do with their field.

Intellectuals Are the Revolutionary Class

In this section Rod Dreher discusses the importance of monitoring intellectual discourse in society, because it is the cultural and intellectual elites who determine the direction and reach of any new ideology. Sociologist James Hunter says that it is not individual genius that becomes a key actor in society, but the network and the "new institutions created out of these networks".

No idea from the masses flourishes without the acceptance and promotion of the elites, who carry it through these "developed networks and powerful institutions." Taking off from Arendt's reminder that 20th century totalitarianism proved how a skilled minority can rule a passive, detached majority, Dreher points out the mistake in dismissing college campus radicals as non-serious threats. Often mocked as "snowflakes" and social justice warriors, Dreher tells the reader that it is they who are radicalizing broader elites in much the same way the Bolsheviks did in pre-revolutionary Russia. There are a number of parallels between today's SJWs and the early Bolsheviks, from their educated, middle-class upbringing to their desperation to identify with something they can believe in and give them purpose, to treating their found ideology as a pseudo-religion.

With much zeal, SJWs are preaching this gospel and transforming institutions into power cells of influence. SJW cultists, as Dreher calls them are intellectuals spreading their gospel by "intellectual agitation" forming their base in universities where their indoctrinated graduates go on to work in pillar institutions of society.

They are interested in seizing power over cultural and not economic production (unlike their Russian predecessors). SJWs have in fact learned to use "bourgeoisie institutions" to transform the world and bring about social change.

An example of this, Dreher says, is the way corporate America took up the LGBT cause and weaved it into branding strategies.

Futuristic Fatalism

Americans need to be aware that much of society may be blind to the country's own instability, which makes it vulnerable to being overtaken by totalitarian ideology.

Institutional loss of faith, divisive, paralyzing politics, declining participation in civic life, debt, widening wealth gap, a shrinking middle class, Church leadership unable to solve the chronic crisis of the young rejecting religious faith, the ubiquity of pornography and the fog of gender identity politics that have put everyone in a haze—all these point to an unstable and weak society ripe for an ideological takeover, given the right catalyst — like a war, economic depression or some other severe and prolonged crisis.

Dreher notes that a collapse followed by a revolutionary reconstruction is a closer threat than people might think. To understand the hypnotic allure of left-wing totalitarianism we must first understand the Myth of Progress that SJWs subscribe to, which drives their fanatical beliefs and is also the reason many people find it hard to say no to SJWs selling this ideology with "confident zealotry". The Myth of Progress is what fuels their fanaticism and feverish utopianism.

CHAPTER THREE

Progressivism as Religion

The Russian art impresario who was being feted by Russian high society after mounting a successful exhibition of portraits he curated from some of Russia's wealthy homes, toasted the age Russia was about to enter without knowing exactly what it was going to be, guided only by the certainty that it was big, and it was at hand and it was going to be glorious and beautiful.

Dreher uses this example to show how naive and mistaken were Russia's young liberal elites about the ideology that was about to put a stronghold on their nation. They were fooled into buying what the Communists were selling which is an ideology that represented the fullest version of what they all worshipped: Progress.

Dreher says "the modern age is built on the Myth of Progress." His use of myth is deliberate in describing Progress as the story woven into our evolution as a society, and that we use it as an anchor to understand our place in society and measure our value against the time we've spent living in it.

Believers of this myth submit to its linearity, which informs its creed—that the present is better than the past and is moving forward, to a future inevitably better than the present. Ergo to stand in the way of progress is to literally move backwards.

Dreher says that to understand how present-day progressives are constantly defeating their opponents, one must fully grasp the Myth of Progress and how communists have manipulated it to suit their agenda.

The Grand March

All left-wing progressives believe humanity is on the Grand March, and is moving towards equality, fraternity, justice, happiness, progress—the future. Progress therefore is absolute and unavoidable. Communism places itself at the head of this March.

So, to stand against the Communist Party as the leaders of this Grand March to a progressive future, is to stand against progress itself. Conversely, it means to stand for everything backward and oppressive because to reject Communist ideology is to reject the future.

Propaganda helped enforce this, recalls Tamas Salyi, a Budapest English teacher who spent his youth in Hungary. He says Communists spread the message that they were "changing the village for the better." He recalls how films would be shown depicting farmers using technological innovations to improve conditions and that anyone who rejected these put their families' lives in danger. The noble end of improving life and the future, is the justification communist rule used to destroy all opposition. For why and who would oppose progress?

Modernity in Progress

Belief in the Myth of Progress is not limited to Marxists and left-wing progressives.

The US as a whole believes in the Myth of Progress and with good reason. Dreher lists the economic and technological advancements America has achieved in its short history as a country and how its ideals have evolved to guarantee civil rights and freedom for all. America is all about progress.

Dreher says Christians subscribe to this too because of its Judeo-Christian roots. Unlike its eastern counterparts that look at history and progress as a cyclical movement, Hebrew defines progress as linear, beginning with creation and travelling forward to ultimately, hopefully, redemption.

He notes however, that not all progress is an improvement on the past, especially when progress is achieved separate from God. He warns of the dangers of progress in a secular context, without guidance from scripture on Man's fallible nature, without respect to God as Creator and judge of everything.

He takes the reader through a quick historical overview of progressivism, which has its beginnings in the 18th century during the Age of Enlightenment, and when its more radical Continental proponents secularized it and replaced faith in God with faith in Man (or specifically faith in science.)

The same age gave birth to positivism, a philosophy that believed science is the source of all authoritative knowledge. Positivists believe that society's history as it evolved is the history of science and technology's advancement. Further, that it brings with it moral advancement, creating a system of values grounded in science instead of cultural traditions and religion.

It shares with Marxists the core belief that science will end all material suffering. Liberal democrats and Marxists have more than this philosophy in common as noted by John Gray, a contemporary philosopher. Positivists promoted the idea that technology produces a "convergence of values" and that it is accepted, uncontested fact today.

Dreher notes that the original American dream, the one carried by Puritan ancestors is anchored in their faith. They wanted to create a world where they were free to worship God. Today that liberty is defined as having the material stability and freedom to determine oneself the way one sees fit.

While the puritan model wanted to use freedom for a Scripture- guided life lived in virtue, the contemporary world view is to use freedom to achieve well-being, led by the sacred Self.

The Myth of Progress empowers people to become who they wish to be, aided by science and technology, and unencumbered by limits imposed by religion and tradition.

Progress is accepted as a moral imperative, and to stand in its way is to stand against change and the natural order of things. And while liberals and conservatives clash on the details of state intervention, and the rate and speed of it, no one challenges its principal belief of allowing man to have enough money and autonomy to do as he wishes.

Progress as Religion

The idea that man is not fated to live a life of misery, poverty and oppression is a revolutionary concept in human history. The promise Marx's communism made gave hope to people who never imagined they could get out of the cycle of suffering traceable to their ancestors. That hope becomes religious zeal, a faith one clings to much as a Christian clings to God for strength and answers.

Marxists are atheists who believe religion blinds the people to their power to change their circumstances by toppling the social order. Marxism promises "radical politics with science and technology that could bring heaven on earth."

Dreher says the ideology of Progress is a perversion of religion which inherently speaks to the "hungry hearts" of humans.

In the past, communism answered a religious longing in people, as noted by Milosz, who were looking for hope and salvation from their suffering. In society today, Dreher says, the same yearning and restlessness can be found in young people, secular and not, who are alienated from church traditions and community.

Hence Christians today need to understand that it's not politics they are resisting but a "rival religion."

He explains further the ideals of Marxism and why it was embraced by Russians with the passion of religious converts. He talks about the utopia it promised, why it hated and routed Christianity and religion in all its forms, and the strength of the revolutionaries' resolve –

which is not unlike the spiritual strength asked of the faithful.

Heresy Hunters in Our Midst

Dreher talks about the concept of "thoughtcrimes" - - an Orwellian term, as it occurs in present day society.

He relays a conversation he had with Sir Roger Scruton, an English intellectual and prominent conservative academic in the UK, who is also, for Dreher, one of the most articulate critics of "political correctness".

Scruton used his own experience to illustrate the dire consequences of having a dissenting opinion today, against anything approved as correct by the Left.

This is how soft totalitarianism has begun operating in modern society. It is especially vicious for people whose occupations involve opinion making, like academics and journalists. "The aim is to prevent your voice from being heard." The punishment for thoughtcrimes can be severe, including losing your job, ostracism, and public humiliation.

From his travels to communist states, Scruton saw that being accused of a thoughtcrime or "heresy", is the same as being convicted. And the punishments were effective in keeping dissent in check and maintaining control with minimal effort. So once in a while new thoughtcrimes would be invented to weed out "enemies of the people."

In Scruton's time it was the Zionist Conspiracy which no one could question because no one knew what it was. In present-day society it is words like "homophobia" "transphobia" "fat-phobia" "ableism" etc. These "heresies", according to Dreher, inform the ideologies behind the soft totalitarianism of our time much as Marxist doctrine informed the ideological thrust of a totalitarian Soviet era.

Dreher says he hears a lot of stories from social and religious conservatives who live "closeted lives" in the workplace, forced to participate in activities that have nothing to do with their jobs or express support for beliefs that run counter to their own, for fear of losing their jobs and reputations if they were ever to express dissent.

This is the face of soft totalitarianism today in American society. Bloodless but no less effective in silencing opposition.

Understanding the Cult of Social Justice

In this section Rod Dreher talks about the menace of SJWs in society and how they depart from their originator -- the Christian Social Justice Warrior, whose work is grounded in faith-based values and Church teachings. He calls SJWs progressive militant zealots whose nature is fundamentally religious.

James Lindsay, an atheist and university mathematician who has spent time studying their behavior in society, says social justice fulfills psychological and social needs that religion once did. He calls SJWs an "ideologically motivated moral community."

Dreher notes that SJWs are not moral relativists but rigorists, puritanical about their beliefs and tolerating no dissent, imposing and enforcing without hesitation.

Some of these beliefs are, according to James Lindsay:

☐   THE CENTRAL FACT OF HUMAN EXISTENCE IS POWER AND HOW IT IS USED

Where everything in life is understood through the lens of power and its dynamics within society. SJWs' want to reorder society to ensure "equitable power relationships". Resistance to SJWs ideology is "practicing hate" which must never be allowed.

☐   THERE IS NO SUCH THING AS OBJECTIVE TRUTH; THERE IS ONLY POWER

Those who have the most power are the arbiters of truth.

☐ IDENTITY POLITICS SORTS OPPRESSED FROM OPPRESSORS

Your identity is the group you belong to.

☐ INTERSECTIONALITY IS SOCIAL JUSTICE ECUMENISM

There is a "matrix of oppression" and people link identities based on group: ergo your identity is also with the group you intersect with.

☐ LANGUAGE CREATES HUMAN REALITIES

SJWs use language and the power of discourse to legitimize or de-legitimize anything, be it an idea or a person. They believe in the power of words to frame human nature and police written speech and thought because anything that offends them is a form of violence.

☐ SOCIAL JUSTICE AND CHRISTIANITY

Where the distinction between Secular social justice and its origins in Christian social justice is differentiated.

The social justice movement of present day SJWs is a perversion of Christian teachings.

For Christians "social order that denies sin" and allows man to be alienated from his creator can never be called just.

Dreher ends this section with a call for Christians to work for social justice grounded firmly in Church teachings and to reject any social justice campaign that implies God is working against man and his happiness.

Back to the Future?

Being nostalgic about the future and romanticizing it is something Americans, a naturally optimistic people, are wont to do. Believing that "everything will work out for the best" is a crippling habit that must be stopped according to Dreher. He uses the example of the Russian impresario who toasted Russia's "beautiful death", never knowing the destruction about to come.

But at the same time, Dreher stresses the importance of Christians remaining hopeful despite all odds.

Soviet communist rule for example, was something most dissidents thought was never going to end. They didn't notice the rusting core of a system that had been decaying for the last eight decades.

Dreher wants the reader to be emboldened, and in talking about the need to stay optimistic in resistance, mentions names like Lech Walesa, Aleksandr Solzhenitsyn, Karol Wojtyla, Václav Havel, and others who came out to stand for truth and justice without the assurance of a victorious end. They did it because it was the right thing to do.

Today, it is hard to stand against a totalitarianism that comes softly, dressed as progressivism for which "progress" means man's desire becoming limitless. But this is what traditional Christians must do in a mass consumerist democracy, unlearn political myths in a culture that no longer argues in broad Christian categories— like the black preachers who led the Civil Rights movement for example, who used the Bible and its language to argue their cause.

Dreher says the landscape now is different and Christians must understand the nature of the opposition in order to put up a real defense against it. SJWs and Leftist Progressivism regards Christians as the final obstacle to the Grand March to progress. The message is that Christian beliefs prevent man from becoming truly free and happy. And Dreher notes the faithful will be continuously tracked and attacked to fulfill the mission of making the world perfect.

CHAPTER FOUR

Capitalism, Woke & Watchful

This chapter is about the relationship between capitalism, surveillance technology and woke ideology that is bringing soft totalitarianism closer to realization than most Americans think.

Dreher starts with a conversation with Kamila Bendova, a resident of Prague who still vividly remembers living under communist rule. Their discussion focuses on how Americans today readily give up personal information via social media platforms, and how many miss the importance of maintaining inviolate, one's private life.

Bendova told Dreher that a zone of privacy is crucial in order to "stay free to speak the truth." She warns that in a totalitarian state, anything can be used against a person. This is why information is power and in history, governments were able to exercise that much more control over a people, because it knows them.

After the Berlin Wall fell, the East Germans opened to their victims, records of its secret police. Historians later discovered that many German citizens were giving information about their neighbors to the State. It was an efficient snitch-system that kept the people in check and the government informed, with little effort.

Dreher makes a comparison to present-day society and how in a theoretical totalitarian takeover, the government won't need a network of neighborhood spies to gain information and insight about the population. Americans live their lives so openly online, the state will just need to check Facebook or Twitter or Instagram, and access the data mined by companies that profile the American consumer, which Americans comply with daily, without thought.

The advance of digital technology, the ubiquity of social media platforms--all these have become tools for surveillance that would make Stalin and Lenin jealous.

The Rise of Woke Capitalism

The rise of Big Government in America was regarded by many conservatives as a necessary evil. The Soviet and its Allies still posed a threat to American democracy mid 21st century, so the normally anti-state conservatives put up with Big Govt., to protect American freedom.

To counter this, they embraced the rise of Big Corp., which was seen by many as a way to control the growth of State power. The end of the Cold War saw liberal world leaders like Clinton and Blair bowing to globalization. And coupled with leaping

67

technological advancement, the last 25 years witnessed a historic rise of corporate power in America.

Now there are mega corporations with greater wealth and power than most countries, and the Internet-powered US have companies like Google, Facebook and Amazon wielding enormous influence over public and private life.

Big Business has eschewed its traditional neutrality when it comes to political and social issues. And more, it has been leaning to the Left, Dreher notes. This began in 2015 when a coalition of mega corps like Apple et al., threatened retaliation against the State of Indiana if it did not reverse course on a bill it passed that would protect businesses from getting sued for anti-gay discrimination. Indiana reversed, which encouraged lobbying from other companies to make other states pass pro-LGBT legislation and reject religious freedom bills.

This heralded the era of Woke Capitalism which has gripped corporate America. Corporate social responsibility, diversity programs and activities, campaigns supporting favored groups like LGBTs, are its markers.

It is Big Business embracing social progressivism, it is the synergy of progressive ideology with commerce and consumerism-- the most potent forces driving America. And using vast resources at their disposal they are sending a message that conservatives and "religious traditionalists are obstacles to the social good."

The Rise of Surveillance Capitalism

In its early years, Google had to figure out what to do with "data exhaust" or surplus data, gathered from individual searches. In 2003, they finally did, by creating and patenting a process which allows them to use the data for target-specific advertising. Thus, "data extraction" became the new business model of the tech economy, as companies like Facebook and Amazon made fortunes processing and selling user data to Big Business.

This is where surveillance capitalism originated.

Harvard Professor Shoshana Zuboff, author of "The Age of Surveillance Capitalism" coined this term and describes it as the relationship of modern American society with Big Business, which married advanced surveillance technology to fulfill its mission to satisfy the material needs and wants of Man.

This technology comes in the form of software in the devices we buy that keep us digitally connected (and trackable) to people, networks and other devices in a bid to make life easier. Alexa, Siri, facial recognition tech, online shopping, GPS and navigation apps, are just some of the examples. Dreher states that a quarter of America's population has sacrificed privacy for convenience. Big Brother has been invited into over 70 million American homes in the form of technology that sees, hears, and makes a record of nearly every aspect of a person's daily life. Consumerism paved the way for Big Brother to gain the love of the American people. It watches, collects and stores data to profile a person, learns how he thinks and behaves, to figure out what he wants today, and to predict what he will want tomorrow and at some point, manipulate and dictate what he will want in the future.

Right now, Big Brother is not a scary government figure, he is a capitalist. He is the face of Big Business, a seller, a maker of human desires and the goods that satisfy them. But this unfettered access to personal data is obviously dangerous, Dreher says. And while it is not obvious, surveillance capitalism is how Big Brother laid the groundwork for soft totalitarianism. It conditions people to accept the invasion of technology in their lives and to see it as normal, never becoming aware of the unseen power of external forces – like giant Left-leaning technocrats --   now have to shape thought and behavior.

The Politics of Surveillance

The advent and ubiquity of surveillance technology is dangerous for the simple reason that an elite group -- whether they are technocrats, or the government controlled by the technocrats -- now have the power to curate thought, promote an ideology or suppress dissent. This power comes from their ability to give or cut off an individual's access to their technology and services, whether it's a social platform like Facebook, YouTube and Twitter, or a service platform like PayPal or an institution like the banking industry.

Surveillance hands an individual's information to a powerful few who can potentially execute

71

judgement on the individual concerned, depending on how aligned that individual is to their own politics, ideologies and beliefs.

Dreher cites many examples of this, from Facebook and YouTube de-platforming users who violate their community standards, to PayPal refusing access to certain groups with conservative politics, to JP Morgan being sued for closing someone's account because of suspected membership of the alt. right, to Citibank announcing it won't do business with gun manufacturers. Even Google has been found to be manipulating search results to present a skewed reality to the searcher.

Dreher cedes that for content sharing platforms like YT and FB, a standard policy is necessary, owing to the evil and unscrupulous entities in the world who will exploit these platforms and promote bad things.

But the question is always who sets these standards of acceptable content? Who determines what thoughts and actions merit policing? It is not a stretch to imagine companies using these mined data to exact punishment on people and groups they find to be politically and socially undesirable, or for

SJWs in roles of corporate leadership to want to manipulate how people act and think.

Dreher presents a foreseeable but theoretical threat. Currently, companies seem only to use these vast amounts of data bought from "surveillance capitalists" to direct consumer behavior towards the wanting and purchasing of things i.e., choosing one brand of soap over another. The danger is when those things and choices become ideologies-- or political candidates.

A small group, whether it is a business led by an SJW or the US government itself -- can decide that suppression of dissent is necessary to push a progressive agenda forward and will find it easy to do so, using the data on hand to identify voices that should be muted.

CHINA: The Mark of the East

An example of a totalitarian state that has managed to synergize surveillance capitalism and communist rule perfectly is the People's Republic of China.

China has become something of a unicorn-- and in the words of journalist John Lanchester, it is on its way to becoming the world's "first AI-powered techno-totalitarian state."

China embraced the model of surveillance capitalism and uses consumer data, biometric information, GPS tracking coordinates, facial recognition, DNA, and other forms of data harvesting to exercise control over its citizens.

In China, most people engage in cashless transactions to buy goods and services, using smart phone apps or facial recognition tech. While this gives safety and convenience for the individual citizen, it has a darker utility. It also provides a steady stream of personal data and information about that citizen, to the government. And this accumulated data is used to profile, track and ultimately execute judgment on a person's movement, behavior and speech.

It also feeds the social credit system-- an ingenuous apparatus created with the aid of surveillance capitalists-- which rewards good behavior and "punishes" bad, via a points system which has real consequences in the daily life of Chinese citizens.

74

Basically, the higher your score the more privileges you enjoy, the lower--well life can be quite uncomfortable. From modes of transport, access to establishments, ability to travel and more, the social credit system is woven into all aspects of daily life. And with it, the government has ensured the people's total compliance to the State. Even when dissidents emerge in the future a system is in place to predict and identify them before they can make any serious impact.

Dreher warns that it won't be difficult to apply the same practices in America, where the people themselves police their own behavior and toe the line drawn by the government.

Can It Happen Here?

The short answer is yes. The technology to monitor people's daily lives is already here and more than that, has been fully integrated and accepted into their lives by the majority of Americans.

The hard totalitarianism China enforces on its people is not likely to get a foothold in the democratic US: American culture is far more individualistic and something of that nature would be met with great political resistance.

However, because Americans have already embraced these surveillance technologies, they can be easily activated and used to serve social justice causes. And if democratic majorities ever believe that government and private power centers in society need to take control to maintain order, it will happen.

Shelter From The Gathering Storm

Rod Dreher ends Part 1 of the book Live Not By Lies (A Manual For Christian Dissidents) by summarizing the most salient points he just spent several chapters discussing. He paints a grim picture of the state of American society today and how vulnerable it is to the forces of soft totalitarianism.

From how ideologies have evolved to become more humanistic, to how man is being driven farther apart

from God and traditional beliefs, to social justice
warriors attacking dissent and making it dangerous
to express faith-based morals, to the example set by
China in giving the modern world a concrete path to
a totalitarian state run by surveillance technology
and capitalism, exploiting man's weakness for
convenience and comfort – all of these and more,
have made the road to resistance as difficult as it
can get for Christians today.

But it must be taken. How does one resist the
coming of soft totalitarianism? This is the subject of
Part Two and the ultimate goal of his book.

PART TWO

How To Live In Truth

CHAPTER FIVE

Value Nothing More Than the Truth

"The Power of the Powerless" is an article written by Vaclav Havel, a Czech playwright and dissident, who ultimately became his country's first post-communist President.

In this, what Dreher calls his most "powerful piece of political writing" Havel addresses his countrymen by exhorting them to resist communist rule by living in truth.

He creates a story about a greengrocer living in a communist state, who puts up a sign at his store that says "Workers Unite"— a famous slogan from the Communist Manifesto. He does this to live in peace, an assurance to the state that he means to conform. It's a lie but he lives with it. Havel then posits the scenario that one day, this same greengrocer snaps and decides to tear down the sign. He begins to act and speak in public in accordance with his conscience. He finds the strength to step out of the lie and "break the rules of the game". He finds his integrity and dignity once more as he rejects the lie and decides to live in truth.

The greengrocer will pay the price for this and will suffer, a lot; his shop will close, he'll lose money, his children's future will be endangered, he is even shunned and persecuted by people around him so they might stay out of trouble.

But he endures all this and keeps living within the truth. And his gesture, Havel says, is not meaningless. In breaking the rules of the game, he revealed to everyone the very fact of the game—the very fact of the lie.

He lifted the veil and did the most dangerous thing of "addressing the world", letting others see what's behind it, and more, that it is possible to live within the truth. Through him, others now see without question the lie that they too are living in.

And Havel says this is important because the lie is only perpetuated with universal belief. Anyone who steps out of it shatters the illusion it wants the people to believe and becomes a threat to the whole system.

What the greengrocer did may have been a small act of rebellion, but such actions can kindle a revolution.

Havel was imprisoned a year after he published this essay. A decade later he became the first post-communist President of his country. Dreher quotes a Russian proverb to encapsulate his message: "One word of truth outweighs the whole world." The challenge today Dreher says, is to live in truth and speak and act to defeat evil. And to do this means to endure the consequences such an act will bring.

Choose A Life Apart From The Crowd

Dreher gives two examples of people who lived in truth during the Soviet era and gladly endured the consequences of such a decision.

Father Kirill Kaleda, one of 6 children of an Orthodox Christian family wanted to study history when he was a young man in Russia. But his father was scared he might be contaminated by Soviet ideology if he were to take up a subject that would inevitably find an intersection point with politics.

His parents were anti-Bolsheviks and, at the time it was the practice to have children of such families study the natural sciences. Father Kirill became a geologist instead.

He refused to join the Komsomol or the Communist Youth League and recalls a time when he lost the dream of an opportunity to travel the world, because travel wasn't permitted for non-Komsomol members. He stayed true to his conscience and recommended a friend instead.

Father Kirill says to live in truth is to accept the limitations that such a choice will put on one's life—professionally, for example.

Dreher tells the story of retired Baptist pastor, Yuri Sipko who told him that in the 1950s when he attended school in Siberia, his teachers got into trouble because he refused to wear a badge with

82

Lenin's face on it and the red scarf of the Young Pioneers, a group for communist youth. He was a Baptist, which was all the reason he needed to reject such articles.

Being a Baptist in Soviet Russia was like being a permanent outsider. Their faith is such that to consider living a lie for the sake of peace is like death.

Sipko talks about the incredible hardships he and his family endured — and still they held to their faith and believed.

Reject Doublethink And Fight For Free Speech

"Doublethink was normal life," according to husband and wife Vladimir Grygorenko and Olga Rusanova, a couple from the Ukraine who migrated to the US in 2000. They talk about how growing up in a culture of lies makes you think that no other way of living could exist—until you realize that there is another way.

They have an appreciation for the freedoms being (now) American provides, having known first-hand what it meant not to have them.

Grygorenko says when a person grows accustomed to living in lies and conforming, he develops a deformed way of thinking, which is why he is concerned that recent polls in the US show waning support for free speech. Grygorenko tells Dreher he can see a growing intolerance for dissent especially among the youth, signaling a society that values the "false peace of conformity to the tensions of liberty."

And this kind of thinking kills a free people. Grygorenko says he has a deep appreciation for the First Amendment and thinks that it should be protected, having come from a country with a meaningless constitution.

Maria Wittner was once sentenced to death by a communist court following her involvement in the 1956 Hungarian uprising. She says it is a duty to fight for the right to speak and write freely, no matter what. She endured many hardships in prison, in large part because of her uncompromising truth-speaking. "It matters that we speak plainly," she once told a prison guard after being scolded for telling the truth. Maria says that living in a world of lies seems inescapable, but we can do something about it. People can refuse to accommodate it.

Dreher says that under soft totalitarianism it is harder to see what price is paid for compromising the conscience. Wittner says it's an individual decision that everyone makes--to live in fear or in "the freedom of the soul."

A free soul brings free thoughts, and free thoughts bring free words.

Cherish Truth-Telling But Be Prudent

In the struggle to combat lies, in the desire to live in truth, sometimes compromise becomes inevitable or the only option. Dreher talks about the wisdom behind choosing the battles worthy of fighting. He warns against rationalization but says prudence is not cowardice.

Tamas Salyi recalls one day when he went home from school in Hungary and told his father about how the Soviets liberated their nation. It was 1963 and 17 years prior, Salyi's father had been linked to a typewriter on which anti-Soviet propaganda had been written. The Scouts connected to that machine were punished severely, from death to exile to internment camps.

And so Salyi's father, upon hearing what his son said, sat him down and gave him the true history of Hungary under Soviet rule. After that he told his son never to speak of what he learned in school.

This is an example of prudent truth telling. Salyi's father wanted his young son to know the truth but was prudent enough to warn him not to say anything about it, wise enough to teach him how to handle it.

In contrast, a much harsher fate came upon Tamas Salyi's father-in-law, Judit Pastor's dad –

a journalist fired for refusing to swear allegiance to the Soviet-installed government following the Soviet invasion in 1956.

In 1968, he was imprisoned after tearing down a poster of Romanian dictator Nicolae Ceaușescu at a trade fair in Budapest. Judit's father was outraged at the persecution of ethnic Hungarians by communist Romania. He got 18 months, was given electroshock therapy 50 times – as it was common practice for political prisoners to be treated like mentally ill patients – and was left a shell of himself.

His life was destroyed, and his story kept secret by the family until now, which was a painful burden for his daughter. She is proud that her son today has taken up the same cause her father died for—the plight of ethnic Hungarians—but reflects that given what was lost over her father's brave yet reckless move, there is value in passive opposition. "Sometimes silence is an act of resistance."

See, Judge, Act

See the lie for what it is. Reject it, teach your children to see it and reject it as well. Further, see the consequences of living with lies and make the decision not to, and to live within the truth.

87

Make a judgement on how you will confront and deal with a lie, should it ever confront you.

Sometimes it will demand that you act out in public – i.e., in defense of someone being slandered. Other times you may need to stay silent. You must remember that prudence is not cowardice, while keeping guard against rationalizing, because that is practicing ketman.

Act to live a life in truth and recognize that to live not by lies is to endure consequences, because there will be some. Act expecting struggle, hardship or suffering. It must be accepted, so accept it. If you cannot accept the act of the greengrocer in the myth, then you may be further down the spiral of the lie than you thought.

CHAPTER SIX

Cultivate Cultural Memory

In this chapter, Dreher talks about the importance of memory, as both witness to historical truths, and warning to the inheriting generations. This is especially crucial in any discussion about totalitarianism, communism, its origins and its proximity to present-day American society.

Dreher begins by relaying a conversation he had with a young woman who, ignorant of the violence and destruction it brought to the world, remarked that communism is beautiful, "this dream of everybody being equal."

He wasn't surprised to discover that she knew nothing of its history and laments that his generation and the ones before, failed hers.

This is proven by the 2019 edition of an annual survey conducted by the Victims of Communism Memorial Foundation. Its task is to determine where most Americans stood on the topics of communism, socialism and Marxism in general.

It found that a good number of Americans from post-Cold War generations had positive views of left-wing radicalism, and only 57% of millennials thought the Declaration of Independence "offers a better guarantee of freedom and equality than the Communist Manifesto."

Dreher mentions Laura Nicolae, a Harvard undergrad who in 2017, wrote in The Harvard Crimson that she and her classmates were getting a one-dimensional, sanitized version of communist history. Milan Kundera, famed Czech novelist and anti-communist, said this is why communists make it a priority to conquer the hearts and minds of the young.

It's important to ensure that younger generations are fully aware of the horrors of a totalitarian society. Their predecessors need to impart their memories, lived experiences and accurate historical information and context about totalitarianism, and how close a threat it still is, even in a country like the US. Because forgetting makes a society vulnerable to totalitarian ideology and a collective loss of historical memory will have a devastating effect on the future.

Why Memory Matters

"How Societies Remember" is a book by the late British social anthropologist Paul Connerton. In it he explains the three different types of memory: historical, which deals with factual events of the past; social, which is defined by personal choice about what the self deems most important to remember and most exhaustively, cultural memory—which is everything about a society that makes up its identity.

Man understands and interacts with the present, informed by and framed against his memories of the past. In this manner, think of society as a person, and culture is its identity. Then think of the people that make up this society as individual holders of memories– artifacts – that are collectively sifted and pieced together to create a story. This story is what becomes cultural memory, and society uses this to remember what it is at all points in time.

Without this collective memory, culture can't exist. Without culture, society — made up of the people who live in it – has no identity. This is why a totalitarian regime forces people to forget their cultural memories.

The ideal, easily conquerable person, says Hannah Arendt, is one who is completely isolated. So, the regime destroys traditions, eradicates religion, controls what is taught in school, imposes its own value system and rewrites history. It needs people to forget their society's true origin-story to make way for a new ideology that becomes the conquered society's new identity.

Ex-communist Polish intellectual Leszek Kołakowski says this reflects "the great ambition of totalitarianism—the total possession and control of human memory."

History has shown that totalitarian states achieve this by controlling information, education and media. Dreher says this can be accomplished even in free countries today, evidenced by the Harvard undergrad's experience—by teaching those who aspire to leadership positions what it is important for them to remember, and what does not matter.

The essence of modernity is the absence of any structure that could hamper man's prime directive which is to exercise the freedom to choose. Connerton says, "To be modern is to be free to choose. There is no sacred order, fixed virtues, and permanent truths. There is only here and now and the eternal flame of human desire. Volo ergo sum— I want, therefore I am."

Christians today find it difficult to pass on the faith to the young in large part because the community has got used to the fact that there so few shared beliefs and customs that transcend individualism. Connerton notes that it is not enough to pass on historical information if you want to keep cultural memory alive. It must be carried by tradition, lived subjectively, embodied in shared social practices— words, certainly, but more importantly, acts.

Create Small Fortresses of Memory

Paweł Skibiński, one of Poland's leading historians, says that before he entered the seminary in 1943, Karol Wojytla was an actor. And when the Nazis arrived in Poland, he and his theatre group knew

93

that it was crucial for the Polish people to resist the forced erasure of their cultural memories, to survive what was coming. Hitler's plan to conquer Poland was the destruction of the two foundations of its identity—a shared Catholic faith and their "sense of self" as a nation.

Wojtyla and company wrote and performed plays about Polish history and their Christian Catholic faith. These were viewed in secret, as discovery by the Gestapo would mean imprisonment or death for both the players and the audiences. This was the greatest weapon the Polish had, to resist the Nazis and the succeeding Soviet form of totalitarianism.

In Poland, Skibiński explains, the only long-lasting social institutions that existed were the church and the family. Communism tried to break the family apart by controlling education, teaching the young to be state-dependent and luring them away from the church using the promise of sexual freedom as bait. Things, he tells Dreher, which Polish people are now seeing happening in the West. He says whereas before they admired and felt like it was a safe place, that is no longer the case for many Poles.

Skibiński focuses on language as a preserver of cultural memory. During that time, communists forbade people to talk about history in unapproved ways. Dreher notes that this is an observable phenomenon today. Liberal progressives, especially in universities, have reinvented language and created new jargon to make propaganda sound more palatable, intelligent, charming even, to conservatives.

Words are assigned values they didn't before have, positive values for terms like "dialogue" and "tolerance" and negative ones for phrases and words like "traditional family" and "hierarchy". Dreher says this abuse of language for ideological use is a habit rooted in Marxism, that of "falsifying language": replacing the meanings of familiar words with new, highly ideological definitions.

And this is important to note because propaganda, among its other evils, can also control what a society deems worth remembering. From Karol Wojytla's example, a way for people to resist totalitarianism's attempts to rewrite cultural memory is by creating small cells of safe spaces where it is okay to speak and embody the truth.

Make the Parallel Polis into Sanctuary Cities

Parallel Polis were underground safe spaces for
social interaction and intellectual discourse, free
from state-control or influence, in communist ruled
Czechoslovakia. Czech mathematician and human
rights activist Václav Benda came up with the idea,
knowing that the public square was no longer a
place for non-communists to have their voices heard.

A key event in parallel polis were seminars held in
private homes where scholars would discuss
prohibited topics. These were fueled by the desire to
preserve cultural memory in the face of annihilation
and in so doing "cultivate seeds of renewal."
Prominent Western intellectuals like Sir Roger
Scruton, philosopher Charles Taylor and literary
critic Jacques Derrida, joined these sessions.

Scruton observed later on that the thing communists
couldn't take away from the Czechs was their zeal
to preserve their cultural inheritance. The Czechs
believed it contained not just their historical
memories but their souls. Czech dissident Jan
Patočka, described these seminars as "the solidarity
of the shattered." They were an act of responsibility
by the old—those who still had their memories of

96

what was real—toward the young, in a bid to keep
the true people and identity of Czechoslovakia from
disappearing.

Bear Communal Witness to Future Generations

Dreher recalls the day he spent in the Butovo Firing
Range, a field in Moscow turned national
monument for the dead, after the Secret Police
under Soviet Rule once massacred over twenty
thousand political prisoners within a span of 14
months during the height of Stalin's Great Terror.

Father Kirill Kaleda tends to this hallowed place,
overseeing it and the nearby church.

Dreher talks about the people he met and broke
bread with on that day, discussing communist era
Russia with those who lived through it.

A man named Vladimir Alexandrovich introduced
himself that day and was curious as to what the
American author was doing in Butovo. Dreher told

him about wanting to learn about communist Russia, because his émigré friends were raising concerns that America seemed headed toward a totalitarian direction. Alexandrovich remarked that it could happen. "History always repeats one way or another."

Father Kirill, over their shared meal, learns of this prediction and agreed that Butovo could happen again. He had just been talking to young students who didn't seem to know anything about the events of Butovo. He laments that propaganda, which did not die with the fall of the Soviet Union, is responsible for this ignorance. Propaganda, happening even now as he talks about the unfolding events in the Ukraine, pitting Russians and Ukrainians against each other. He says young people now have a duty to go beyond what they watch on TV or read in papers. A responsibility to look for the truth. Because propaganda can erase cultural memories, and the way to combat it is to bear witness to history.

This is the essential point of this section, highlighting the importance of remembering the events of history and passing it to the younger generations. Much like how Dreher bore communal witness when Russians gathered that day in Butovo, to read aloud the names of the dead.

See, Judge, Act

See memory as a weapon for cultural defense. That history goes beyond what is written in books because it is in the stories we tell ourselves, in the memories we hold that tell us who we are. See that history is in everything we do, say, observe. History is culture and so is Christianity.

Make a judgment that the way for Christianity to survive is to recognize the importance of memory and the role of culture in preserving and transmitting the faith and its practices. Know that one must embrace and support tradition in defense against the new social order the elites want to legitimize.

Act and be inspired by the examples of the heroes of history like Pope John Paul II and

Vaclav Benda who found ways to fight for the preservation of cultural memory.

Tell stories in all the forms available to us but never forget to manifest cultural memory in communal deeds. Revive the practice of private seminars on humanities subjects, celebrate festivals, perform concerts, make pilgrimages, learn traditional cooking — these are examples of communal activities we can do in shared resistance to a paradigm that dismisses the past as insignificant.

Do not underestimate the importance of ordinary, everyday things within the home, such as Christians sharing traditions, praying, talking about God, the Bible and Church history.

CHAPTER SEVEN

Families Are Resistance Cells

Dreher opens this chapter by painting a weakened picture of the American family today.

Unlike its Christian dissident counterparts in former communist states, the American home is not a refuge due to loosened family ties and the traditional commitment to marriage.

It is unfortunate that US Christians, Dreher notes, are not much different from unbelievers.

This chapter talks about the family as the strongest cell of resistance in society and Dreher cites three which are model examples of Christian families living in truth today.

The first family are the Bendas of Prague, a large Catholic clan whose patriarch was imprisoned for four years by Czechoslovakia for being a human rights activist.

The Family and the Totalitarian State

The Bendas are much beloved in Prague for their fight against communism. Vaclav Benda (parallel polis) and his wife Kamila were academics and devout Catholics living in a country that was mostly secular. They were also the only Christian believers working at the top level of the Czech dissident movement.

Vaclav Benda believed that the family was the "bedrock of civilization" and must be protected. Deeply troubled about the threat communism posed to the family, he thought about what role it could play in the anti-communist movement.

In an essay called "The Family and the Totalitarian State" Vaclav talks about how to help the family endure a government and social order intent on destroying it. He says there are three gifts in the Christian model of marriage and family that believers can cling to when struggling within a totalitarian order.

➤   the fruitful fellowship of love - mutual need and nothing else, is enough to forge bonds of affection with our neighbors.

➤   freedom - keeping true to marital vows and staying faithful through whatever obstacles allows us to defy and transcend our own finite human nature and we are elevated higher than angels to God.

➢ the dignity of the individual within family fellowship - the law of love is greater than the demands of justice between spouses, between children and their parents. This makes us irreplaceable in the roles we play in the family; and even when love fails, we are saved by our shared responsibility, allowing us not to give up on erring members.

Much like when communist rule attacked the family as a social unit for fear that it was a threat to the State's control of the people, today the traditional family is attacked by the woke Left which seeks to dismantle it as an oppressive institution.

The consumerism that has overtaken modern society has reduced the family's role to producing "autonomous consumers", accountable to nothing but to their own desires which must be satisfied at all costs. This is why Benda's advice for families in a totalitarian state remains relevant. He lays out several ruling principles that would serve any Christian family going through hardship.

a)   divorce should not be an easy solution for difficulties

b)   don't let children mock the sanctity of marriage with their own relationship choices

c)   respect for life is sacrosanct (no to abortion)

d)   the father is first and foremost a servant of Christ

e)   the family house must be a real home, a loving haven from which adventures can begin and to which one may safely return at any time.

A Benda Guide to Child-Raising

Rod Dreher had the opportunity to interview the children of Vaclav and Kamila when he visited the latter to pay his respects to her late husband.

The Benda couple reared children who all kept to the faith under communist persecution and are all, including the grandchildren, practicing Catholics today. Dreher wanted to know how they brought up children under the most testing of conditions, with such strength that their faith remains unassailable,

and with understanding for their parents' youthful
mission and the sacrifices that came with it. Here is
their advice:

MODEL MORAL COURAGE

For the Benda children, no one was a greater
example than their father who they likened to the
Sheriff in High Noon, a movie they watched
frequently as children. Their father took the time to
explain to them what was happening in their society,
taught them the difference between dictatorship and
totalitarianism and gave them rules that they
understood to be for the safety of the whole family.
These children of dissidents didn't have the luxury
of rebellion, and son Patrik says they had to set
aside disagreements to fight the outside threat of
communism. Through their father's example they
learned the value of serving something greater than
themselves.

FILL THEIR MORAL IMAGINATIONS WITH THE GOOD

When they were growing up, Kamila read to her
children aloud, for 2-3 hours a day, daily.

The family favorite was Lord of the Rings by Tolkien because the story felt like theirs.

The battle between good and evil was something they understood intimately. Patrik says their mom always encouraged their imagination through books and games. She said it was something no one can ever take away from them.

DON'T BE AFRAID TO BE WEIRD IN SOCIETY'S EYES

The Benda kids were always different, because they were Christian and because they wore strange hand-me-down clothes from relatives. But they never minded it, thinking that to be different was an asset. The Benda kids were raised not to mind what other people said, immunizing them from communist ideology. "They don't go along just to get along. " A valuable lesson, when resisting propaganda and widespread conformity to the totalitarian system.

PREPARE TO MAKE GREAT SACRIFICES FOR THE GREATER GOOD

Kamila told Dreher that her husband once wrote to her from prison to relay the news that the government was considering setting him free if he agreed to move to the West. Kamila wrote him back and said no, that it was better for him to stay in prison and keep fighting. It was a great sacrifice as she was a single mother raising 6 children, a Catholic in a largely secular country under communist rule. But she endured because yielding would betray the dictates of their conscience. And once more Vaclav set an example for his children to follow. Today, the letters he sent to his wife and family while imprisoned are like catechism for his progeny, a testament to the strength of his faith, made all the more impactful because they were penned by a flesh and blood hero.

TEACH THEM THAT THEY ARE PART OF A WIDER MOVEMENT

The Bendas were founding members of Charter 77, the main Czech dissident group at the time. The Benda children participated in the movement, even carrying secret messages for their parents because they would attract less suspicion. Kamila says they were made to feel that as a family they were all fighting the same cause. They also exposed their children to people with views and values different from their own. Many members of Charter 77 were atheists and the only thing they shared was the desire to fight back against communist totalitarian forces. Early on the Benda kids learned how to interact and listen to dissenting opinion.

PRACTICE HOSPITALITY AND SERVE OTHERS

Kamila says being a Christian means standing up for the persecuted, regardless of their faith. And the children were witness to the kindness , strength and compassion their mother shared with the daily stream of people dropping into their Prague apartment looking for advice and comfort, before they went to be interrogated by the secret police.

As adults, the Benda kids have also continued the tradition their parents began when they hosted secret seminars in their home during the communist era.

The Social Importance of Family

Yuri Sipko, one of 12 children, is a Baptist living in Russia. Baptists are rare in Russia, emerging only in the latter half of the 19th century and today are still a minority at less than 80 thousand believers in a population of 145 million. Sipko was once the leader of his country's Baptists which, during the time of communist rule, was a challenge.

Baptists were marginalized and persecuted even by other faiths. They were depicted as a cult by Communist propaganda. But Yuri Sipko credits his parents for having planted seeds of courage in his heart. He admired his father who was the pastor of their congregation when he was a child and wanted to be like him. When his father was imprisoned for 5 years for preaching, their community rallied around their family, and other mothers helped raise him and his siblings. Sipko recalls a time when his teacher called his mother in because he refused to accept lessons in atheism. The teacher said all manner of insults to humiliate his mother, but all she did was take out her Bible and began to read. Sipko found the courage his mother shared with him to stand up to the teacher and proclaim his belief in God.

Yet another example, the much harsher fate that befell Father Jerzy Popieluszko, chaplain to Solidarity which was Poland's trade union. He was killed by the secret police in 1984, his body dumped in a river, for speaking out against the regime. He became a national hero, his funeral attended by nearly one million mourners.

Pawel Keska who directs the museum named after the martyred priest, told Dreher that Father Jerzy's childhood and life before finding his calling in Solidarity, was nothing extraordinary. He

recalls having visited his childhood home which had been turned into a museum of sorts and described the small, nondescript house in a poor village in the middle of nowhere. There was nothing remarkable about any of it except a small piece of paper lying on a small table that bore Father Jerzy's brother's handwriting. "Every day near the table we were praying with our mother." The great destiny that he fulfilled began in a home much like any other, where you find at the heart, a family that prayed together.

See, Judge, Act

See how Christian families today need to take the threat of soft totalitarianism seriously, and Christian parents must lead their families in a more serious, focused, intentioned way.

Christians can't be passive within their families, acting like every other family with the exception of Sunday worship. Judge what needs to change within the family dynamics to mount a genuine resistance to soft totalitarian ideology.

110

Taking inspiration from the Benda family, parents must be discerning about the influences they let through the door. Judge the spiritual strength of each family member and the ability to hold true to Christian beliefs in the face of soft totalitarian ideologies.

Act in service of others, like the Bendas who opened to the world because they were confident in their disciplined, moral, intellectual and spiritual lives. They knew their role was to be of service to their church, community and the world.

CHAPTER EIGHT

Religion, the Bedrock of Resistance

In this chapter, Rod Dreher gives examples of Christian dissidents who suffered and went through harrowing ordeals in the name of living in truth under communist totalitarian rule. More importantly, how they leaned heavily on their faith to get through it. Through these living testimonies to the power of faith, Dreher makes the argument that would seem intuitive to any Christian: resistance in any and all its forms, must be anchored on faith, to triumph.

Dreher shares that all the Christian dissidents he spoke with had one thing in common: they all exuded a deep inner peace which they attributed to their faith. Religion gives the Christian dissident his golden dream, his purpose. This is the fuel that keeps him enduring amidst the hardest suffering. What religion brings to anti-totalitarian resistance is a reason to die—for as one dissident said in the next section, nothing is more beautiful than to die for God, which is a reason to live and survive whatever hardship is thrown one's way.

The Spiritual Exercises of the Prisoner Krcméry

Dr Silvester Krcmery was a disciple of Father Kolakovic and was sent to prison in 1951. Years of training with Kolakovic prepared him for a long prison term, but the conviction that anchored and kept him sane through years of enduring torture and imprisonment was the belief that nothing could be more beautiful than laying down one's life for God.

It gave him the mental strength as well as the spiritual perspective from which to receive whatever suffering he was about to receive, knowing that enduring it brought him closer to salvation.

He kept his hope and his mind, through years of torture, beatings and confinement – by practicing his faith rigorously, memorizing the scripture, evangelizing others and meditating on the words of God. In his memoir "This Saved Us" he wrote that he realized the only way he would make it through was to rely on his faith, not reason. He likened himself to Peter, deciding "to close his eyes and throw himself into the sea." He plunged himself into spiritual and physical uncertainty and knew only faith in God could guarantee his safety.

When he was released 13 years later, he immediately got into the work of rebuilding the underground Catholic church, a movement that was the legacy of Father Kolakovic. Dr Krcmery became one of Kolakovic's greatest and most important followers and was a leader in the Candle Revolution of 1988.

The Power of the Powerless Church

Dreher gives the reader a few examples of Christian dissidents who found incredible spiritual strength in fellowship with other Christians, bearing witness to the true power of a Church rendered powerless by the communist State.

Father Dimitry Dudko was a Russian Orthodox priest who spent 8 years inside the gulag before he was ordained, for writing a poem critical of Lenin. In grief with what was happening to his motherland, Father Dimitry began using his homilies to speak against Soviet rule, taking the people's suffering to the public sphere of the Catholic pulpit.

When the church, controlled by the KGB asked him to stop, he continued his piercing sermons in his home. Word spread in Moscow about the priest who bravely talked about the need for people to cultivate hope that things would get better, that they must "embrace the suffering and love them into healing."

People from all walks and faiths began coming to listen to his talks— people who knew they were living a lie because of the system and were suffering because of it. They were drawn to those who were living in the light of truth.

Patrick Parkinson, an Evangelical Christian and law school dean in Australia, lived in Bratislava as a youth and personally witnessed the power of the underground church movement. In dark times, the Church was a source of strength and hope for people and he recalls his young Catholic friends who would meet in secret every day for Bible study and prayer, always at great risk.

Alexander Ogorodnikov created independent discussion groups. Once a popular Soviet youth leader he became disillusioned with communism and decided to serve the church. He referred to the seminars as passionate expressions of faith.

Viktor Popkov was a Russian youth who went to one of these meetings in the 1970s, despite being an atheist. He found his way to God through Albert Camus' "The Stranger" and despite the risks and trouble attending those meetings at the time could cause him, he said that experiencing the faith gave you a new feeling you wouldn't be willing to give up.

He likened the feeling of finding a living connection to Christ to falling in love and finding the courage to do things you've never done before. For Popkov, that meant putting up with years of harassment from the secret police before landing a 1980 prison sentence. For him, the only way to find the strength for resistance is to have the willingness to die for the faith and principles you confess.

Miracle of the Cigarettes

Alexander Ogorodnikov relates an astonishing story of an unlikely miracle that happened to him while in prison. He told Dreher that when he first arrived at the Soviet prison, the other inmates, upon discovering he was a Christian, told him to prove God's existence. If God gave them cigarettes, they would all believe in Him.

Ogorodnikov told them that while cigarettes defiled their bodies as temples for the Lord, he also felt that God would grant them the small mercy of cigarettes to ease their suffering. He invited them to stand together and pray with him for this. They laughed at him but were respectful as they watched him do precisely that. For the next 15 minutes Ogorodnikov led a cell filled with inmates into prayer, asking for cigarettes. When it ended, a guard opened the cell and suddenly threw a bunch of cigarettes at the group.

He told Dreher that was his sign that God had a mission for him in that prison.

See, Judge, Act

See that in today's world, Christians who practice a passive or superficial expression of the faith will not survive the coming soft totalitarianism. Christians must dig deep in scripture and Church tradition to understand how materialism and individualism have come to compete with religion.

Resistance must come from a more active and focused practice of the faith.

Make a judgment of how current world values and demands have affected our lives and examine whether we are actually followers.

Act to know and be aware of the cost to faithful
Christians. The post Christian world will grow
increasingly intolerant of uncompromising faith-
based values, and the strength of the Christian
dissident's commitment to traditional Christianity
will determine if the world breaks you or if your
faith will build you a fortress made of rocks
impenetrable to the enemy.

CHAPTER NINE

Standing In Solidarity

Rod Dreher visited an old house in Bratislava that
was once the HQ for the print and distribution of the
Christian samizdat, or underground religious
literature prohibited by the regime.

His guide, Ján Šimulčik, a Slovak historian, took
him took him to the basement which had a secret
door that led to a tunnel which had a secret exit that
led to a tiny room containing a printing machine
that produced the samizdat for distribution
throughout communist Slovakia. Šimulčik then

talked about an elevator repairman at the university he attended, who he later discovered worked on the samizdat project at the same time.

It was a testament to how wide the operation's network was and how clandestinely they moved. The Christian underground movement tried to protect its members as best it could. No one knew who was working on what specifically in the movement, to prevent exposure in case one was captured by the secret police and broke under interrogation. Information was shared on a need-to-know basis.

Šimulčik told Dreher everyone took great risks to maintain the samizdat operation. But it was worth it because he, like many others, found meaning in the underground church through the small communities it formed. It filled the hunger people like him had for freedom, truth and knowledge about their faith which their outside world could not give.

The experience of freedom gave them a sense of duty, that they were serving God by serving the people, as well as the courage to continue and eventually do bigger things, like participate in the Candle Demonstration.

Small Communities Can Rescue the Lone
Individual

František Mikloško, a central leader in the second
wave of the Slovak underground church, affirms the
power of the small communities. He tells Dreher
what then underground Catholic Czech Bishop Ján
Chryzostom Korec said, that while the regime can
take everything else like the samizdat or their ability
to speak publicly, what they can never take are the
small communities.

He talked about being in the first community
established by Jukl and Krčméry in 1966 when he
was a university student in Bratislava and how they
began to grow in numbers as word about the
community spread to other towns in Slovakia. By
1988 it was such a large network of believers the
state couldn't do anything to stop it, which had been
the goal from the start.

Mikloško tells Dreher that watching their leaders
act so fearlessly inspired their own courage.

Dreher uses the candle lighting ritual at Easter as a
metaphor for the movement that eventually toppled
communism in the country. It begins in darkness
where a priest takes the flame from the paschal
candle and lights a few held by the believers around
him, who in turn spread the flame to everyone else
in the room until every candle in a chapel of a
handful or a church of hundreds or a cathedral with
thousands – is lit.

Mikloško believes the young of today have it harder,
because it is harder to know who the enemy is. To
them he advises staying true to oneself and to one's
conscience. More importantly, be in like-minded
communities to share the faith with. "We were
saved by small communities."

Solidarity is Not Exclusively Christian

In communist era Czechoslovakia, Christian
dissidents kept friendships with secular dissidents
because there was strength in numbers. Ján
Čarnogurský, a Slovak lawyer who defended
Christian dissidents says at the time it was
important to make allies where you could because
there were not a lot of anti-communists to begin
with.

Miklosko notes that it's also important to maintain an open communication with the secular world as a way to enrich and strengthen one's own faith and a means to stay connected to those who at some point may seek the faith. In the past secular and Christian dissidents shared the belief that communism was a destructive lie. But while it may be true that many secular liberals believe it is justifiable and necessary to oppress religious views, Miklosko argues that good faith liberals have something to learn and something to teach traditional Christians.

Making Grief Easier To Carry

Small communities, fellowships, groups, clubs -- any space one can create and share with others-- is crucial in fighting social atomization and loneliness, which are fertile breeding grounds for totalitarian ideology. Many Christian communist dissidents who went through incredible suffering during the resistance found solace and strength in sharing that grief with others.

Vakhtang Mikeladze is a documentary filmmaker from Germany who was arrested with his sister as a teenager after their father was executed for offending Stalin and branded a traitor. The night they were taken he noticed other vehicles on the road carrying other prisoners and in that moment he and his sister smiled in shared relief that they were not alone.

He wept in shame at this recollection. But Dreher says it only highlights how important "camaraderie in travail" is to survive an ordeal.

Maria Komaromi, observing her own college students in Budapest, says loneliness is a problem especially for the young and social media only masks it. The first step is acknowledging it to counteract it, through the formation of small communities.

This is based on her own experience of her and her husband hosting sessions with young Christians at their apartment during the communist years.

Sir Roger Scruton believes participating in small communities lets a person see their own value in relation to the world and instills discipline from having a sense of accountability to others as well as shared purpose.

Organize Now While You Still Can

Zofia Romaszewska is a fierce human rights activist, a communist dissident in the 1960s and a true hero of modern Poland. She founded the underground Solidarity radio station with her late husband in the 1980s. She is still a force at 80 years old, and she tells Dreher she can see that soft totalitarianism is coming fast.

She exhorts the young to get offline and start meeting face to face. She emphasizes the importance of true solidarity, that asks you not necessarily to give your life to someone, but to have something in common and do things together.

This is the essence of the community that is needed to combat what is coming.

See, Judge, Act

See that social atomization has led to isolation and loneliness, which makes people vulnerable to control and manipulation.

Christians should remember there is spiritual strength in solidarity, in community and fellowship, and reject "social disintegration" as the new normal. Learn from anti-communist dissidents who affirm this is the only way resistance becomes possible for the faithful.

People must form and nurture these communities now, while still living in a free society, because organization becomes harder and more dangerous during a time of persecution.

Judge well, on who to form small communities with and who are worthy of trust. It's a nuanced process and must be handled on a case-by-case basis.

Action starts now while we are still living freely. Following the example of Father Kolakovic, Christians can learn how to create and run underground cells and networks to mount an effective resistance during times of persecution.

Connect with people from all faiths, or no faith and learn from each other. Group leaders should be willing and able to carry out duties and tasks usually reserved for the institutional Church and prepare to step into catechetical, ministerial, and organizational roles.

CHAPTER TEN

The Gift of Suffering

In the final chapter of Rod Dreher's Live Not By Lies (A Manual For Christian Dissidents) he talks about suffering, and how people in modern society have misunderstood its intrinsic value in human life.

Through the experiences of Christian dissidents under Soviet rule who lived in truth, resisted totalitarianism and endured unimaginable horrors in the gulags in the name of faith, Dreher shows how suffering has been their gift, inspiration and ultimately salvation.

He references Huxley's "Brave New World" character John the Savage, who was outcast from the world that believes any hardship in life is a form of oppression that must be rejected.

The Savage, Dreher explains, was "fighting for his right to be unhappy."

A NY Times survey in 2019 showed 4 out of 5 young Americans counted self-fulfillment as a key to a good life and only a minority put value on religion, patriotism and having children.

"This is the generation who will embrace soft totalitarianism."

Young Christians who won't be able to resist for they have been raised in a world that believes that for life to be good it must be free from suffering, "in a Christianity without tears."

Suffering As Testimony to the Truth

People must learn the lessons from Christian dissidents who survived the communist rule, in order to prepare for the trials brought by soft totalitarianism. Hard totalitarianism conquered through fear of pain. Its softer version will conquer through fear of discomfort. And while there is no comparing the level of suffering experienced by Christian survivors of communist rule, it is reasonable to conclude that if American Christians today crumble in their faith at the smallest trial, there is no way they will stand up to a more severe form of persecution in the future. Yuri Sipko says if one is not willing to die for Christ then it's all hypocrisy.

He says the reason so many of the faithful endured unimaginable pain during the communist era was because their willingness to suffer for Christ is "their testimony of the reality of their unseen God."

Their pain makes their faith real to people and reveals to all who witness them, that this world is a lie.

Maria Komaromi says suffering is what makes one authentic. Without it, what you believe in is mere ideology. Suffering is a seal on one's belief that

128

other people can see and be made to think that it is real.

Maria Wittner witnessed horrors during her months spent on death row when she was imprisoned at twenty years old. She spoke of how prisoners acted on the day of their execution, to the number of executions that would take place in a day and how she fainted on the day they executed her friend. Later she realized that she was spared for this purpose, to tell people what she experienced and bear witness to the cruelty of communism.

Admirers or Disciples?

Dreher makes a distinction between an admirer and a follower--or a true disciple of Christ-- using a Terrence Malick film called "A Hidden Life".

It is based on the true story of Franz Jägerstätter, an Austrian Catholic farmer who refused to serve Adolf Hitler. Yet why was he the only one in a village of Catholics who found the courage to stand up for the faith? In the film, Franz talks to an artist who paints Biblical stories. As he ponders on his paintings that give comfort to people but don't lead to repentance or conversion, he provides the answer in the insight that, people like him "create admirers and not followers."

An admirer is someone who will sing the praises of Christ, take comfort from prayer, accept Christian teaching -- yet not risk anything real, not change anything concrete in his life to prove it.

Philosopher Soren Kierkegaard noted that following Jesus is a way of life and not an ideology. Discipleship means becoming one with Him, completely imbibing His teachings. But the admirer makes no real sacrifices, has no skin in the game, and operates on a superficial level.

The follower simply "aspires to be what he admires", knows the cost of true discipleship and is willing to pay it if the need arises.

Suffer Without Bitterness

One of the greatest disciples of Father Kolkovic and instrumental in rebuilding the underground Church movement in Slovakia was Dr Silvester Krčméry. He spent many years in prison and endured much suffering, but he found spiritual strength from the belief that there was nothing more magnificent than dying for God.

He was convinced God was putting him through agony for a reason and that he was a vessel God used to help others endure. He saw his pain as a gift and offered it for the sake of the Church. He found a meaningful existence inside the gulags helping other prisoners by sharing each other's burdens and thus making them easier to bear. None of the suffering he endured for ten years embittered him or made him seek revenge. He continued serving his faith in Bratislava and was true to his promise to the persecutors "to never live in hate, nor rebel, nor complain, for that is where their strength and superiority lie."

"Bless You, Prison" – Receive Suffering As A Gift

The title of this section is inspired by a passage from "The Gulag Archipelago" by Alexander Solzhenitsyn who, after suffering inhuman conditions in prison, remarked upon his release "Bless you prison for coming into my life."

It speaks to the truth of the nature of suffering, as revealed through the life of Christ, that when received correctly, can be a gift. And while the Church does not ask the faithful to seek out suffering, it asks us to endure it with courage if it comes into one's life.

The suffering endured by dissident Alexander Ogorodnikov, proves this.

A communist supporter in his youth, he changed in his 20s and found the faith. He was imprisoned and though he wasn't sentenced to death, he was sent to death row as a form of psychological punishment. But he found strength and purpose by giving comfort to the inmates, offering them a shred of peace and hope during their final days.

He wasn't a priest, but offered to hear their confessions, with the promise of witnessing their repentance when he died and faced God. He was put in solitary confinement as a result of this, where he experienced mystical visions. He would be woken in the middle of the night by a gentle, unseen force. Then he would see the jail corridor and the guards escorting an inmate to be executed. He would see the prisoner from behind, never his face, and would find a sense of peace. He felt it was God saying his and the prisoner's prayers were heard, and that the inmate was forgiven. These visions didn't come for every prisoner and he intuited that not all who confessed their sins were truly repentant.

He often wondered why he was never allowed to see the inmate's face in these visions until the old prison guard assigned to him broke down one night. He told him a horrific story of when he was a younger guard, seeing twenty or thirty priests executed by Russian soldiers in a dark field. They were shot one by one after each refused to deny Christ. The faces of those priests had haunted the old prison guard for years and that night Ogorodnikov witnessed him break. He realized then that God had spared him by not letting him see the faces of the inmates in those night visions. It would have likely driven him to madness as well.

Expect the Worst, Show Mercy to the Broken

This section talks about incidents of unimaginable
torture and suffering inflicted upon the clergy
during the Soviet occupation of the deeply religious
country of Romania, centered around the testimony
of Romanian political prisoner and Lutheran priest,
Richard Wurmbrand.

Wurmbrand testified to what transpired inside the
Piteşti prison in Romania. The "Piteşti Experiment"
was a state-run operation with the goal of re-
engineering the human soul.

The prison was a house of horrors, its occupants,
political prisoners including clergy, subjected to
unspeakable acts of torture and degradation. The
intent was to annihilate them in mind and spirit, so
they be remade obedient citizens of the People's
Republic.

Wurmbrand was an inmate at this prison from 1948
to 1964. He spoke of how the communists
performed all manner of physical torture. He
recalled an incident of a young priest who was tied

to a cross, and twice daily soldiers would force prisoners to urinate and defecate on him after which they would raise the cross and taunt the Christ covered in filth. They were sadistic beyond imagining. They asked another priest to perform the holy mass upon a plate of excrement and urine which the other inmates were forced by beatings into taking for communion.

Wurmbrand asked the priest how he could do it and he recalls the priest was half-mad and begged him for mercy.

Let the Weakness of Others Make You Stronger

Wurmbrand's fellow innate at Pitești, Father George Calciu, was an Orthodox Christian medical student who eventually became a priest. He tells the story of Constantine Oprisan, a prisoner he met when he was transferred to Jilava, an underground prison in Russia.

Oprisan had tuberculosis and was at death's door. He was weak, emaciated, coughed constantly and could barely move. But every word he spoke was about Christ. He was like a saint, Father Calciu says, and he took care of Oprisan's every need, feeding him and washing his body. He was completely dependent on the inmates, but they felt they were being supported by the strength of this weak and dying man's faith. When Oprisan died, they all felt that something had died in them. Galciu says taking care of Oprisan in the final year of his life allowed him to "see the light of God." It was strange but faith-ordained, that while languishing in prison in a dark and cramped cell filled with filth and despair, Father Galciu and the other inmates experienced moments of sublime happiness they had never felt in the free world while Oprisan was alive. He was the embodiment of everything good and loving and they all learned and got strength from him, the physically weakest man in the room.

A Christianity for the Days to Come

There is no comparison between the faith of the past which endured much suffering through witnessing, to the faith of modern society anchored on therapeutic culture, politicized Christian factions and "prosperity gospel".

The latter will crumble in the face of the slightest persecution.

We must absorb the stories of the past, these accounts of faith witnessing through struggle, so that the present can learn and prepare for the future. Who we are as Christians today will determine what kind of Christians we will be when we are tested.

See, Judge, Act

See the value of suffering, and how it speaks to the core of the Christian faith as its essential teaching. Resistance to the coming totalitarianism depends on how we understand and embrace this truth.

Judging the right approach to suffering is a nuanced process. Father Kaleda emphasizes that the Church does not want believers to seek it, for even Jesus in Gethsemane asked God to take His pain away if He so willed. We don't ask for suffering but accept and endure pain and loss if it ever comes and asks us to stand for God.

137

We should learn from the stories of Christian martyrs and believers who gladly suffered for the faith throughout the ages and teach these to our children so they become part of Christianity's cultural memory.

Have faith that God has a purpose for every instance of suffering we embrace for Him, though we may not always know it.

Act to accept suffering and allow it to change you. Suffering is part of the human condition and no one can avoid it. But the lessons of the past and the experiences of the faithful believers teach us how to face it when it arrives. Learn to do that now, during a time of peace. It will determine how we will act in a time of persecution.

CONCLUSION

Live Not By Lies

By way of concluding the book Live Not By Lies (A Manual for Christian Dissidents), author Rod Dreher tells the story of Timo Kriska, a young Slovak photographer and filmmaker who travelled around his country a few years ago to take photographs of survivors of Soviet communism.

Kriska tells Dreher that what stunned him during these encounters, more than their stories of persecution, was the inner peace that each one radiated. They found liberation in their suffering. Their strength grew in direct proportion to what they had endured. And Kriska tells Dreher that meeting them was a transformative experience.

His understanding of freedom changed, and as a result his project took on a new meaning. He found heroes and not victims, and instead of the piece he was creating to remember an unjust past, he began looking in their experiences for a message for the present.

The message was simple: how modern society defines freedom today is wrong. That the notion that man's liberation comes from removing binding commitments like faith and family is "a road to hell."

That in current times, the only force intent on correcting and fighting this is traditional Christianity.

And that's when Kriska realized—in much the same way that faith was seen by the communist past as the obstacle to total control of the people, so too are the forces of soft totalitarianism today, preaching to everyone that religion is the true oppressor of Man. And both tried to suppress and destroy traditional Christian faith.

Kriska knew his generation held fast to the belief that suffering was something you escape from, and his own life was marked with ease and professional success. Yet his happiness did not rise to meet that equally. From his meetings with the Christian dissidents, he realized that suffering could be a gift, that it could be the source of freedom and strength. It is an invitation to share in the power to change, resist and revolt against oppression. And the greatest oppressor, in fact the totalitarian ruler that must be defeated--is the self.

We rule our conscience, we control how we respond to a therapeutic culture. This is the core of soft totalitarianism, to defeat believers with promises of a life free from suffering, that seduces us to surrender to a Christianity without tears.

But living in truth means accepting suffering as a part of life. Truth can't be separated from tears. And the cost of liberty is vigilance over our own hearts.

God's Saboteurs

Marek Benda of the Benda clan of communist fighters and who fought as a teenager against communism with his parents, says that "a single generation always stands between us and tyranny."

The fight for freedom is endless, because we never learn from the past. We see history unfold yet stay blind when it begins to repeat itself right in front of us.

Rod Dreher ends with a call to the reader to act while there is still time. His hope is that the accounts of history will peel off our blinders and galvanize Christians into action.

Thank You!

Hope you've enjoyed your reading experience.

We here at Genius Reads will always strive to deliver to you the highest quality guides.

So, I'd like to thank you for supporting us and reading until the very end.

Before you go, would you mind leaving us a review on Amazon?

It will mean a lot to us and support us in creating high-quality guides for you in the future.

Warmly yours,

The **Genius Reads** Team

Manufactured by Amazon.ca
Bolton, ON